CHRISTMAS MOVIE MAGIC

15 ENCHANTING FILM FAVORITES

ARRANGED BY PHILLIP KEVEREN

ISBN 978-1-5400-9320-2

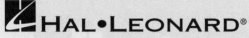

HAL•LEONARD®

Visit Hal Leonard Online at
www.halleonard.com

Visit Phillip at
www.phillipkeveren.com

Contact us:
Hal Leonard
7777 West Bluemound Road
Milwaukee, WI 53213
Email: info@halleonard.com

In Europe, contact:
Hal Leonard Europe Limited
42 Wigmore Street
Marylebone, London, W1U 2RN
Email: info@halleonardeurope.com

In Australia, contact:
Hal Leonard Australia Pty. Ltd.
4 Lentara Court
Cheltenham, Victoria, 3192 Australia
Email: info@halleonard.com.au

PREFACE

Movies can be magical. Christmas movies can be really magical! The songs that are introduced or featured in our favorite Christmas movies become part of the joy of the holiday season every year. All of the selections in this collection carry special memories for me, and I hope you enjoy playing them at the piano.

Merry Movie Christmas!

Sincerely,

Phillip Keveren

CONTENTS

BELIEVE
from Warner Bros. Pictures' THE POLAR EXPRESS

Words and Music by GLEN BALLARD
and ALAN SILVESTRI
Arranged by Phillip Keveren

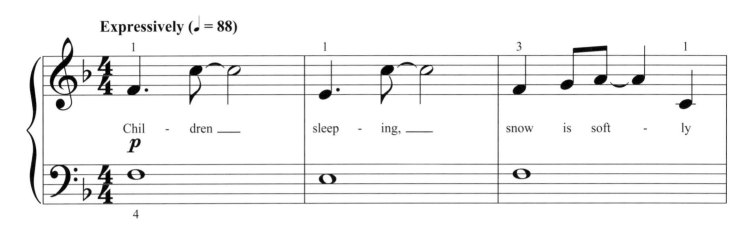

Children sleeping, snow is soft - ly

fall - ing. Dreams are call - ing

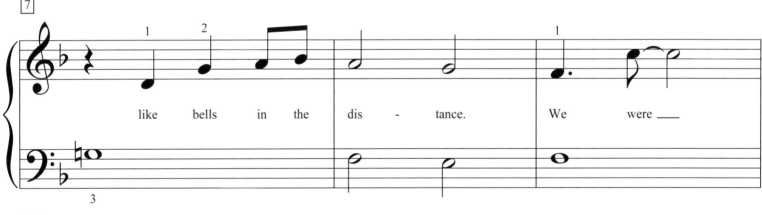

like bells in the dis - tance. We were

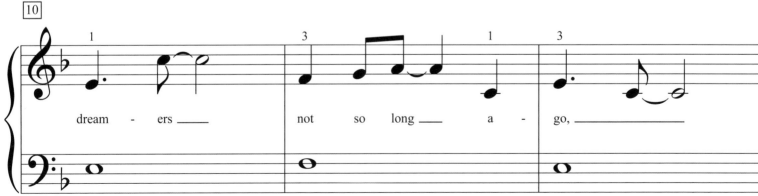

dream - ers not so long a - go,

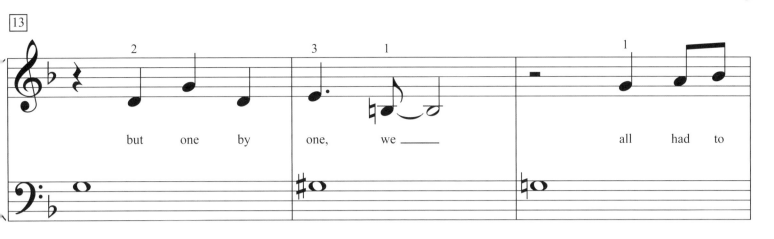

but one by one, we _____ all had to

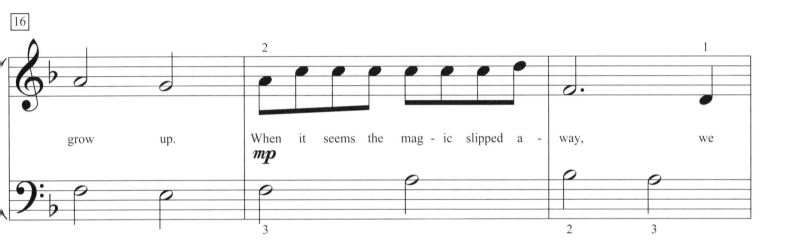

grow up. When it seems the mag - ic slipped a - way, we

find it all a - gain on Christ - mas Day. Be -

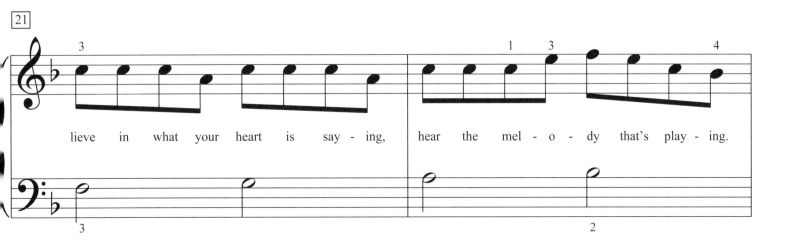

lieve in what your heart is say - ing, hear the mel - o - dy that's play - ing.

23

There's no time to waste, there's so much to cel - e - brate. Be -

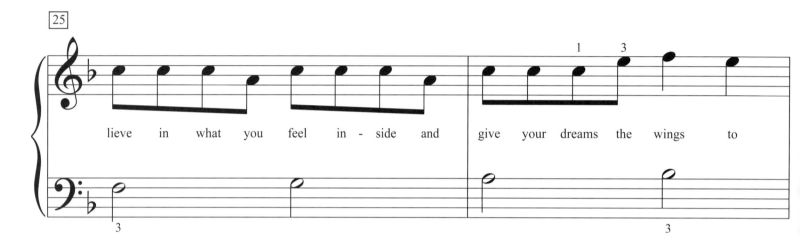

25

lieve in what you feel in - side and give your dreams the wings to

27

fly. You have ev - 'ry - thing you need, if you just be -

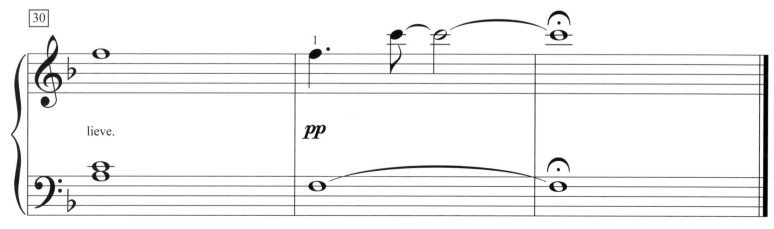

30

lieve.

pp

HAVE YOURSELF A MERRY LITTLE CHRISTMAS

from MEET ME IN ST. LOUIS

Words and Music by HUGH MARTIN
and RALPH BLANE
Arranged by Phillip Keveren

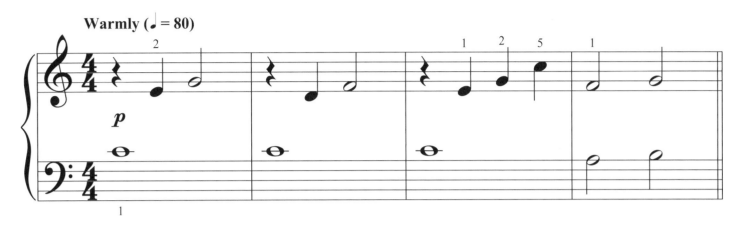

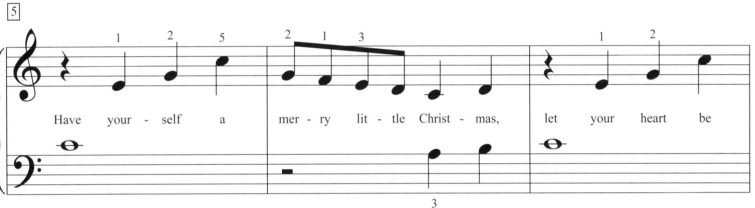

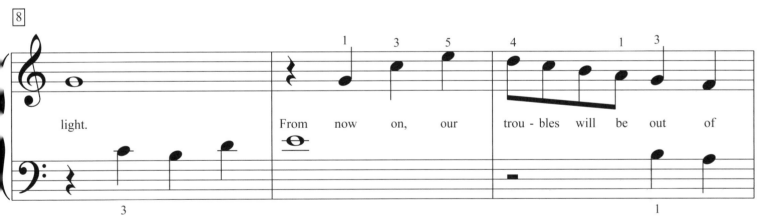

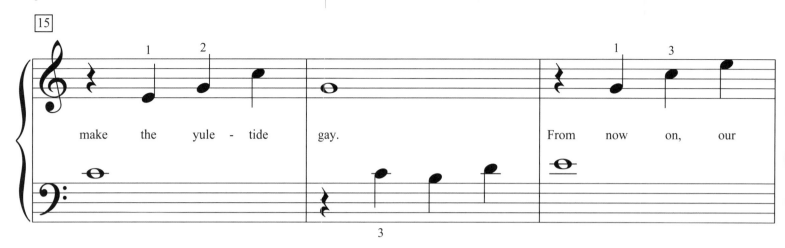

make the yule - tide gay. From now on, our

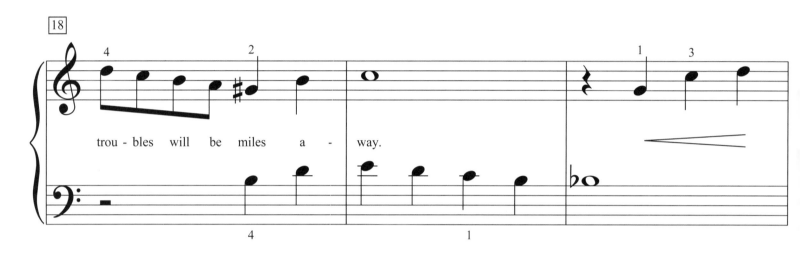

trou - bles will be miles a - way.

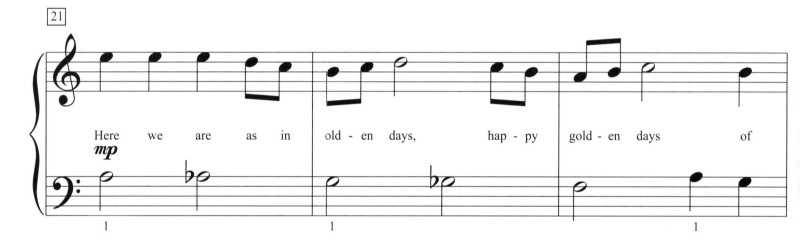

Here we are as in old - en days, hap - py gold - en days of

mp

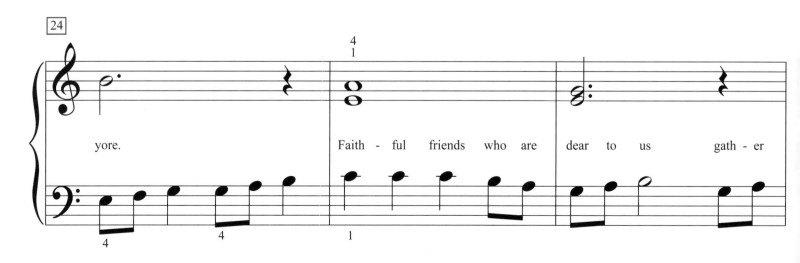

yore. Faith - ful friends who are dear to us gath - er

near to us once more. Through the years we

all will be to-geth-er, if the fates al-low.

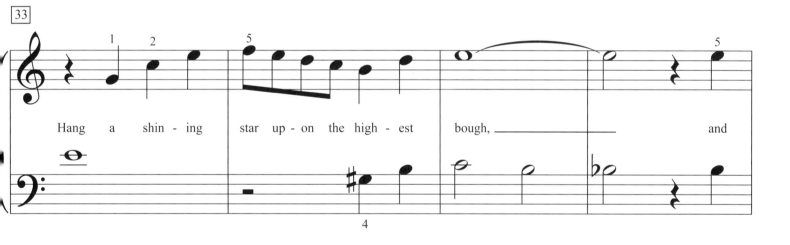

Hang a shin-ing star up-on the high-est bough, and

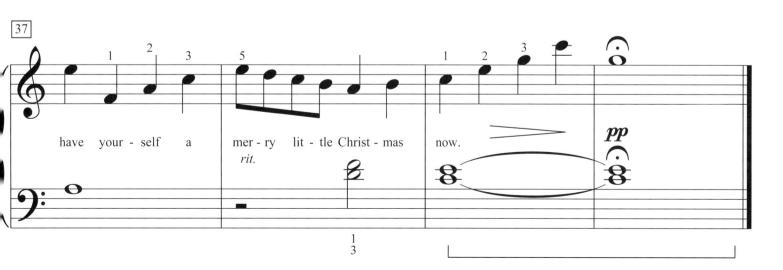

have your-self a mer-ry lit-tle Christ-mas now.

COUNT YOUR BLESSINGS INSTEAD OF SHEEP

from the Motion Picture Irving Berlin's WHITE CHRISTMAS

Words and Music by
IRVING BERLIN
Arranged by Phillip Keveren

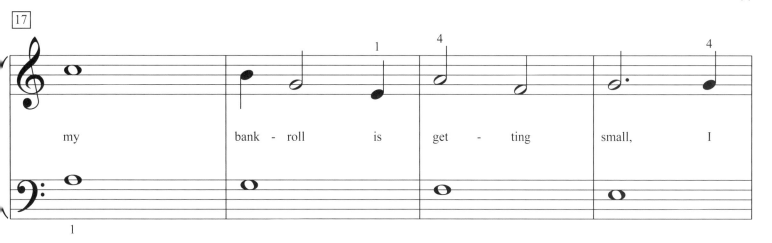

my   bank - roll   is   get - ting   small,   I

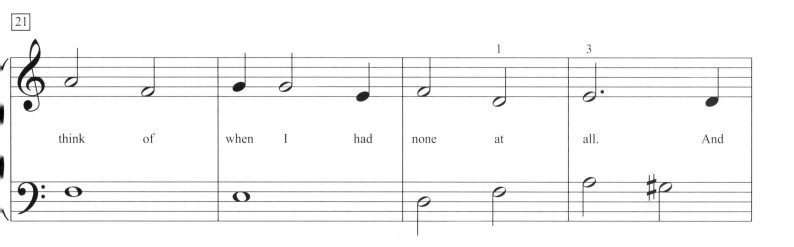

think   of   when   I   had   none   at   all.   And

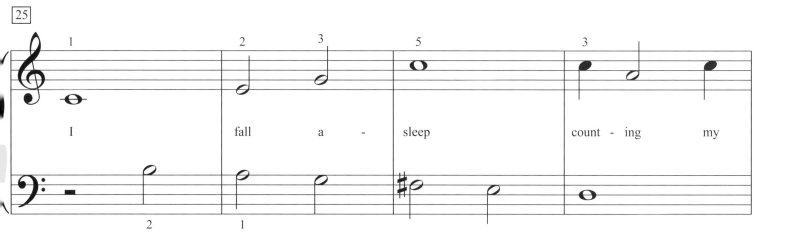

I   fall   a -   sleep   count - ing   my

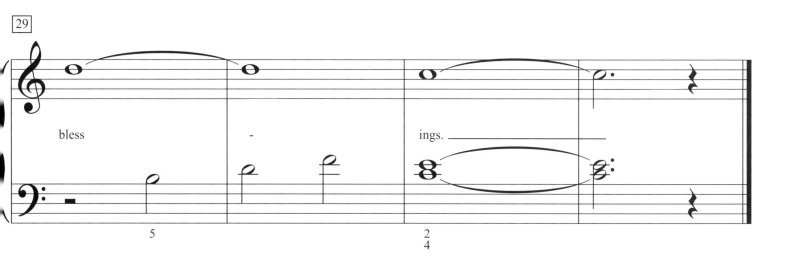

bless - ings.

DO YOU WANT TO BUILD
A SNOWMAN?

from FROZEN

Music and Lyrics by KRISTEN ANDERSON-LOPEZ
and ROBERT LOPEZ
Arranged by Phillip Keveren

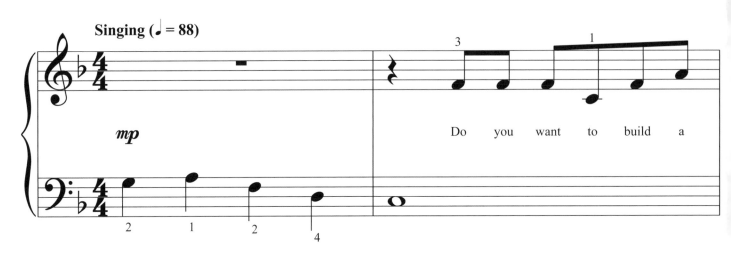

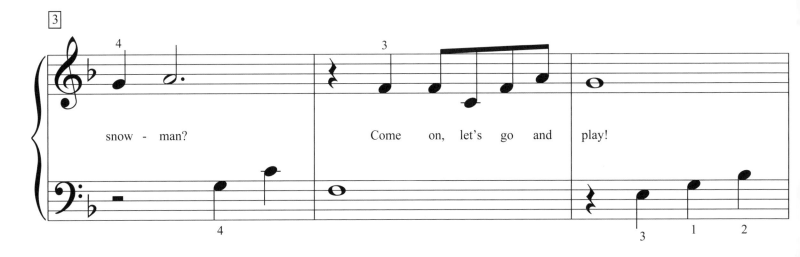

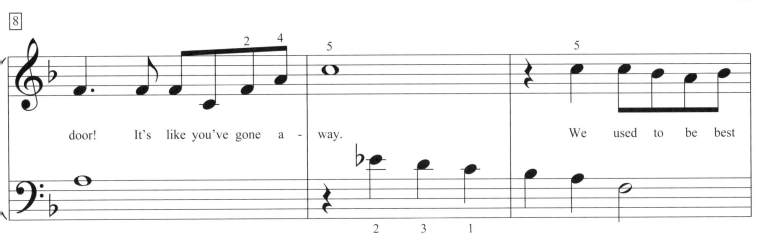

EVACUATING LONDON

from THE CHRONICLES OF NARNIA: THE LION, THE WITCH AND THE WARDROBE

Music by HARRY GREGSON-WILLIAMS
Arranged by Phillip Keveren

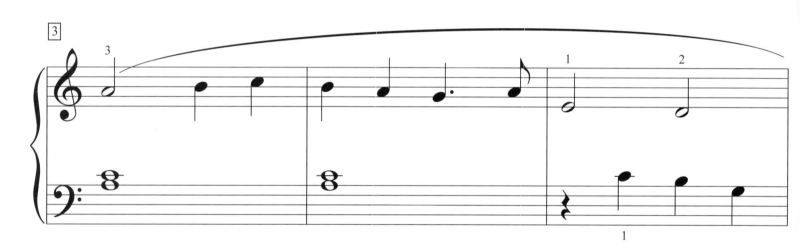

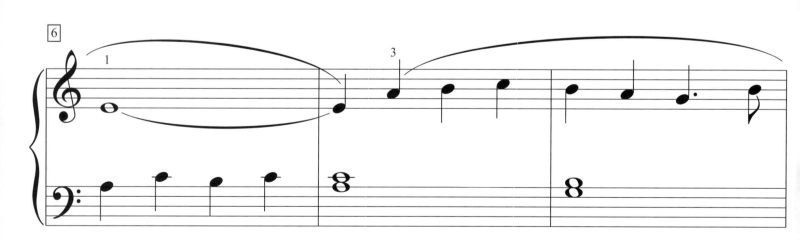

GLASGOW LOVE THEME

from LOVE ACTUALLY

By CRAIG ARMSTRONG
Arranged by Phillip Keveren

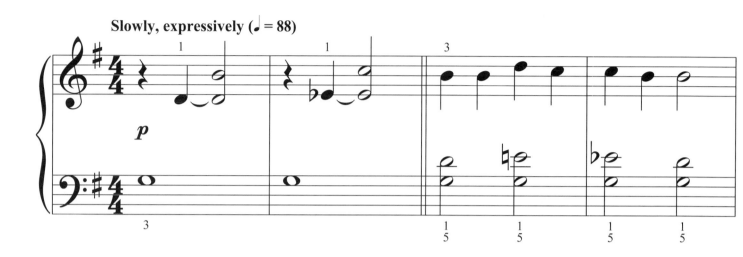

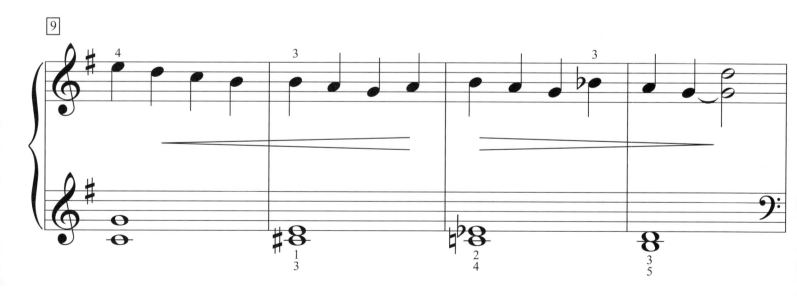

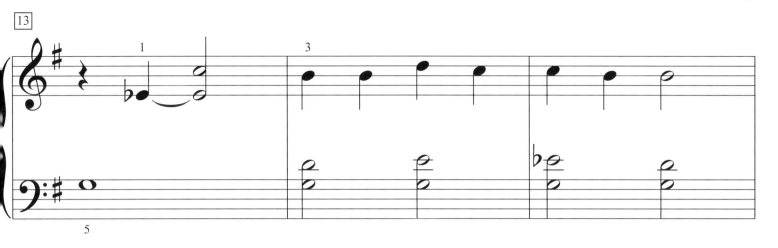

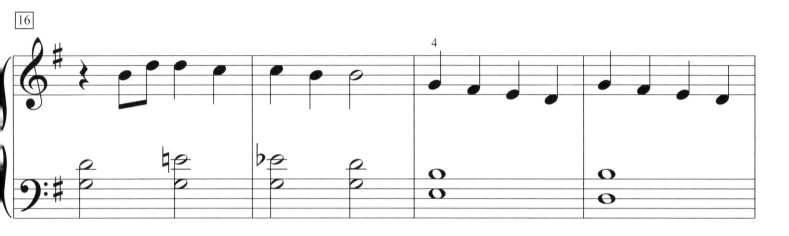

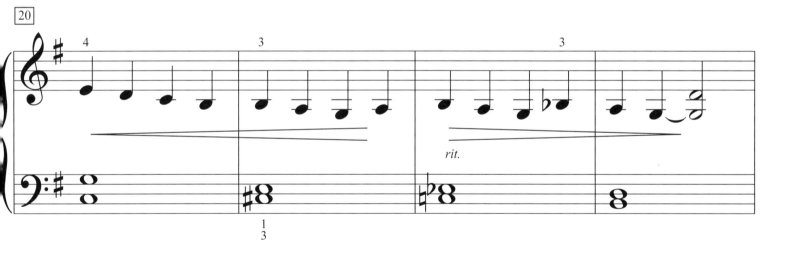

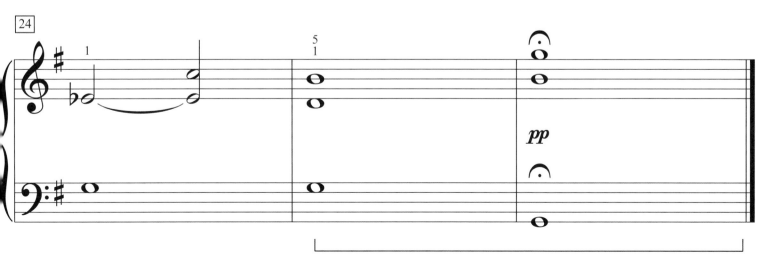

GOD BLESS US EVERYONE
from A CHRISTMAS CAROL

Words and Music by ALAN SILVESTRI
and GLEN BALLARD
Arranged by Phillip Keveren

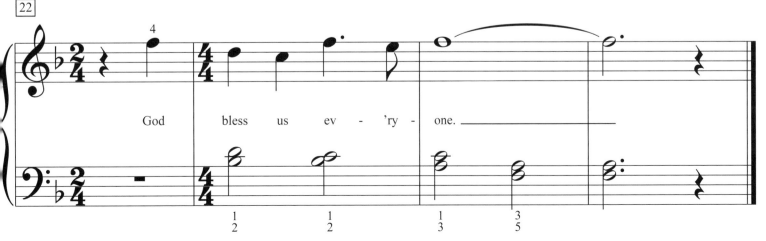

SALLY'S SONG
from THE NIGHTMARE BEFORE CHRISTMAS

Music and Lyrics by
DANNY ELFMAN
Arranged by Phillip Keveren

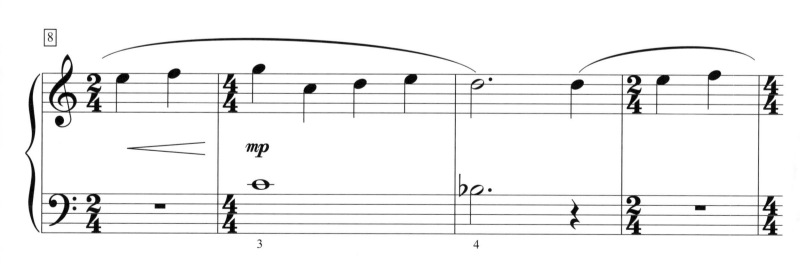

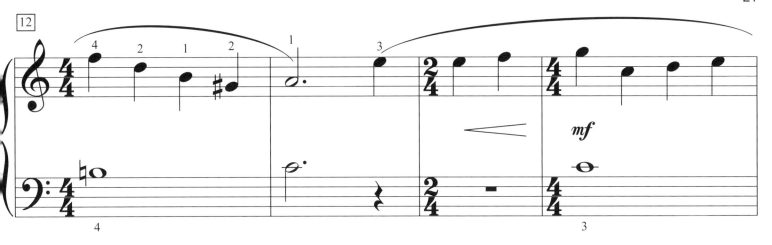

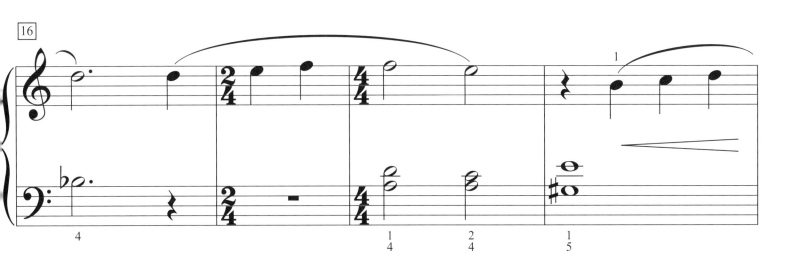

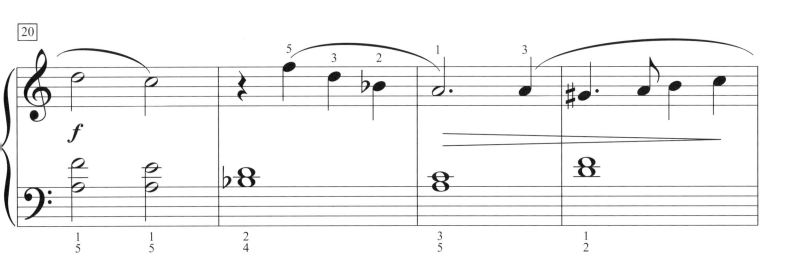

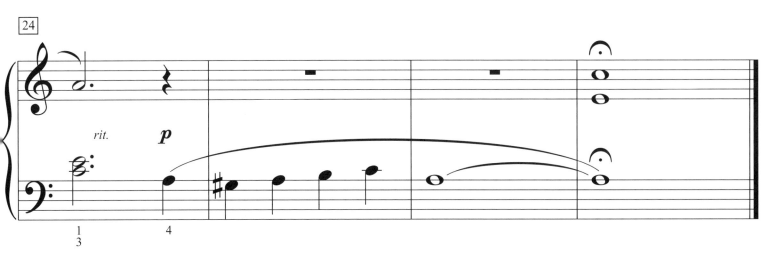

SISTERS
from the Motion Picture Irving Berlin's WHITE CHRISTMAS

Words and Music by
IRVING BERLIN
Arranged by Phillip Keveren

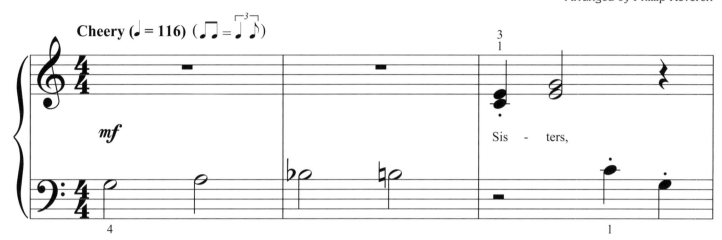

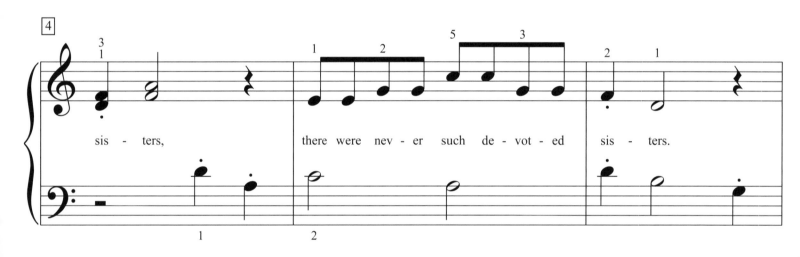

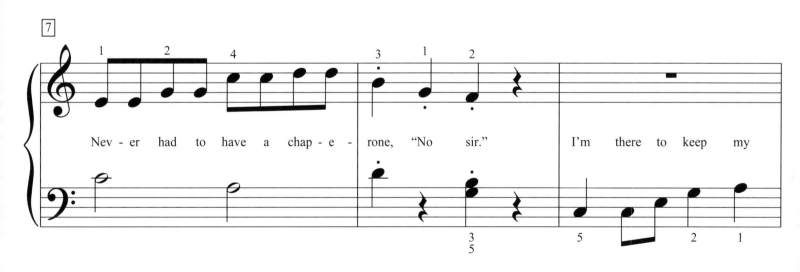

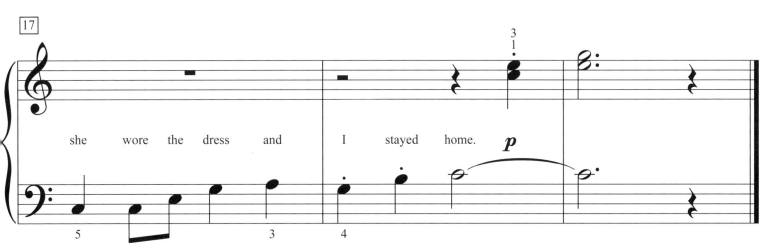

SKATING
from A CHARLIE BROWN CHRISTMAS

By VINCE GUARALDI
Arranged by Phillip Keveren

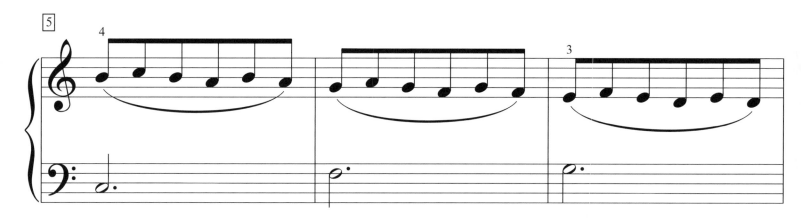

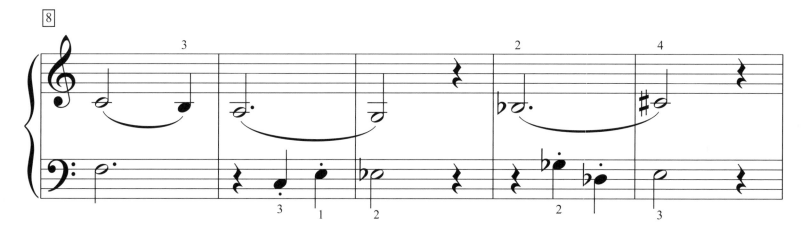

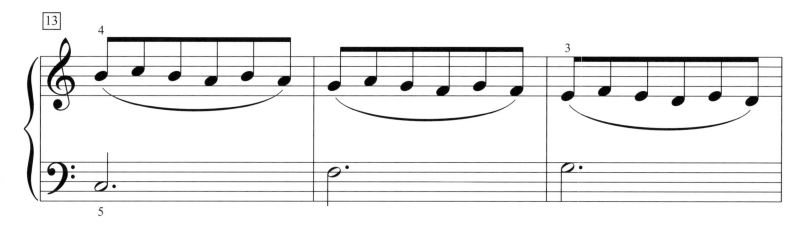

SOMEWHERE IN MY MEMORY
from the Twentieth Century Fox Motion Picture HOME ALONE

Words by LESLIE BRICUSSE
Music by JOHN WILLIAMS
Arranged by Phillip Keveren

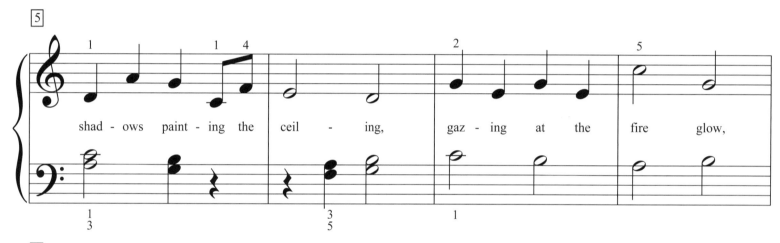

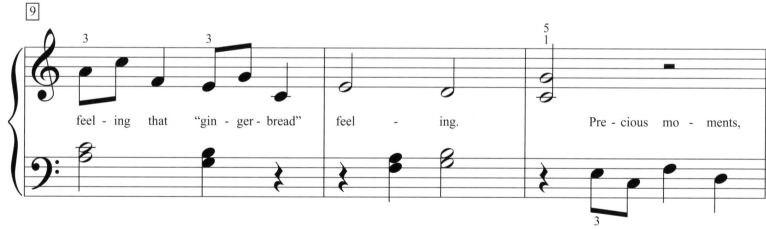

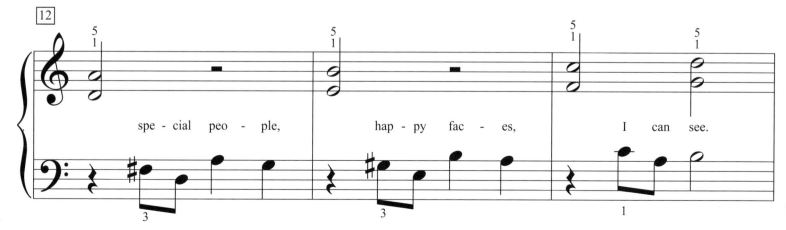

STAR OF BETHLEHEM
from the Twentieth Century Fox Motion Picture HOME ALONE

Words by LESLIE BRICUSSE
Music by JOHN WILLIAMS
Arranged by Phillip Keveren

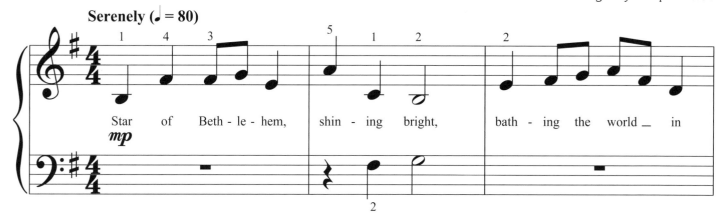

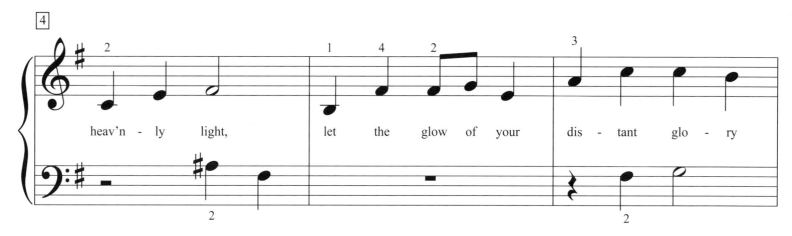

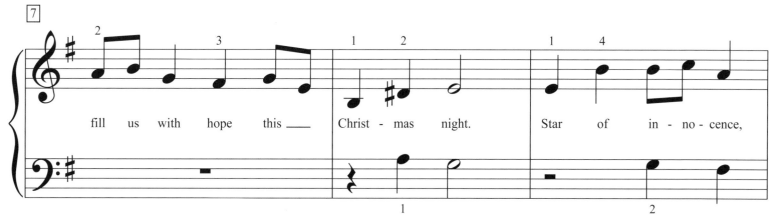

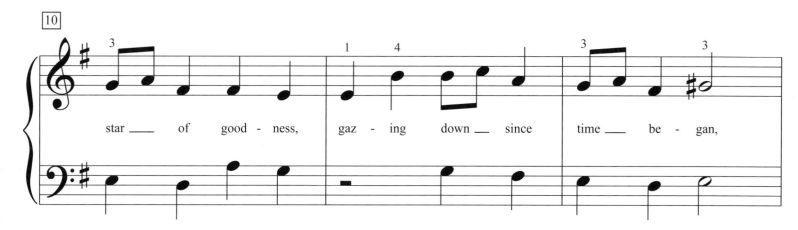

WHERE ARE YOU CHRISTMAS?

from DR. SEUSS' HOW THE GRINCH STOLE CHRISTMAS

Words and Music by WILL JENNINGS,
JAMES HORNER and MARIAH CAREY
Arranged by Phillip Keveren

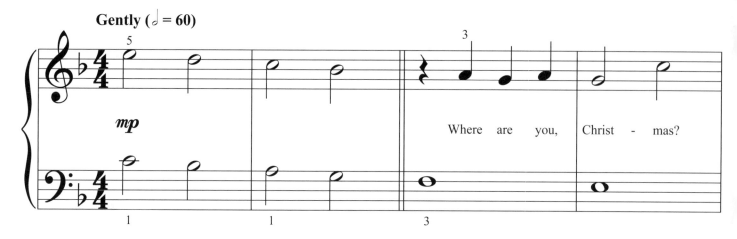

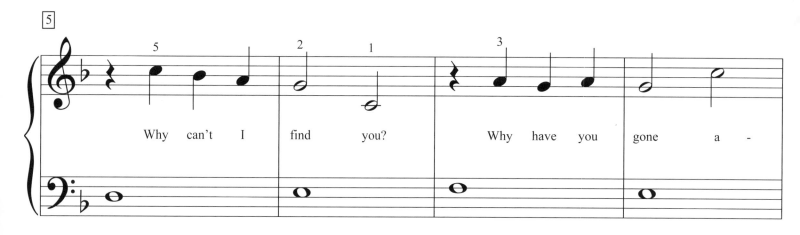

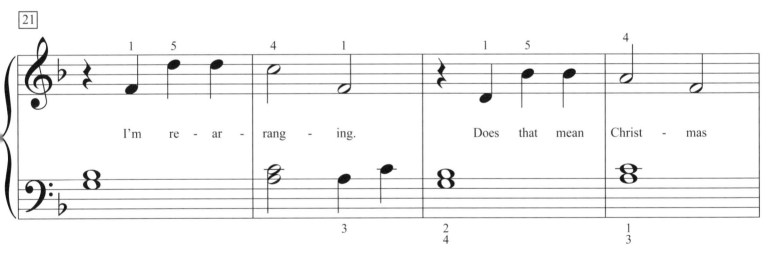

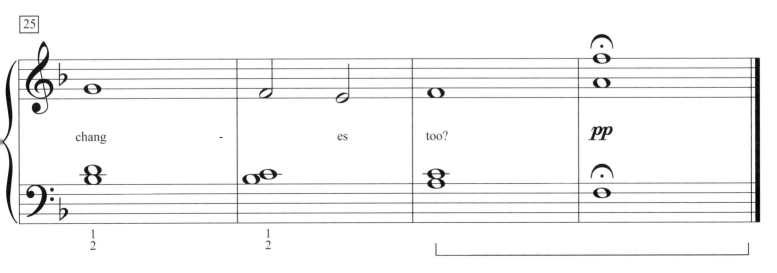

YOU'RE A MEAN ONE, MR. GRINCH

from DR. SEUSS' HOW THE GRINCH STOLE CHRISTMAS

Lyrics by DR. SEUSS
Music by ALBERT HAGUE
Arranged by Phillip Keveren

You're a mon - ster, Mis - ter Grinch! Your ___

heart's an emp - ty hole. Your brain is full of spi - ders, you've got

gar - lic in your soul, Mis - ter Grinch! ___ I would-n't touch you with a

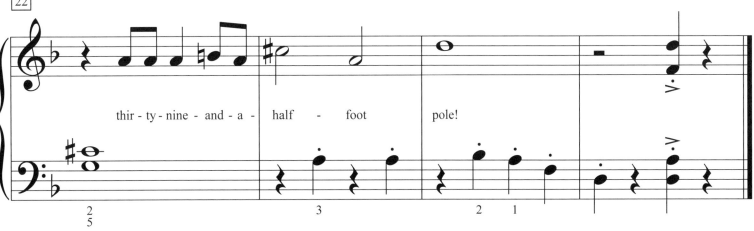

thir - ty - nine - and - a - half - foot pole!

HOT CHOCOLATE
from Warner Bros. Pictures' THE POLAR EXPRESS

Words and Music by GLEN BALLARD
and ALAN SILVESTRI
Arranged by Phillip Keveren

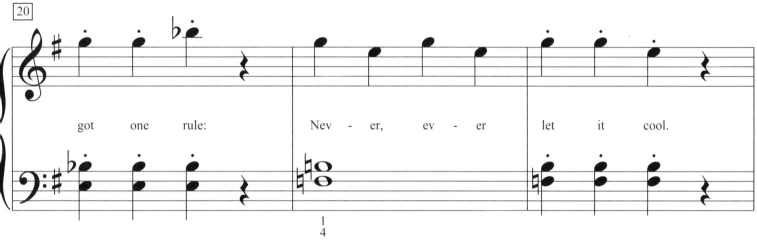

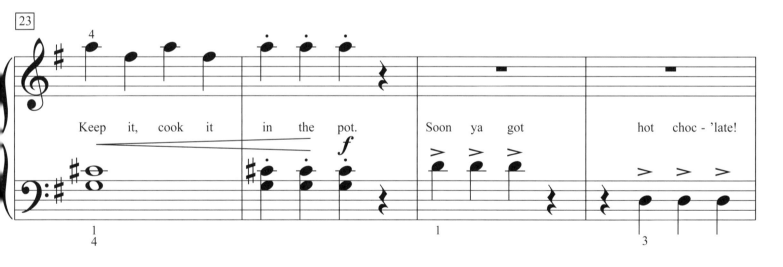

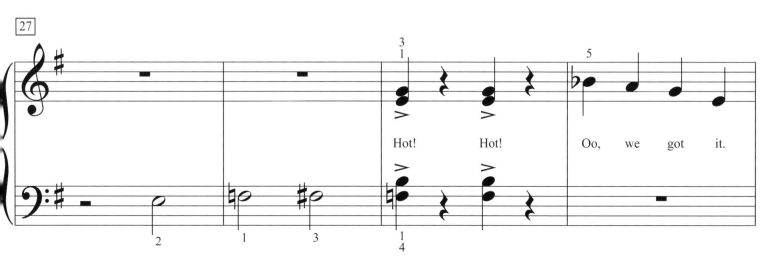

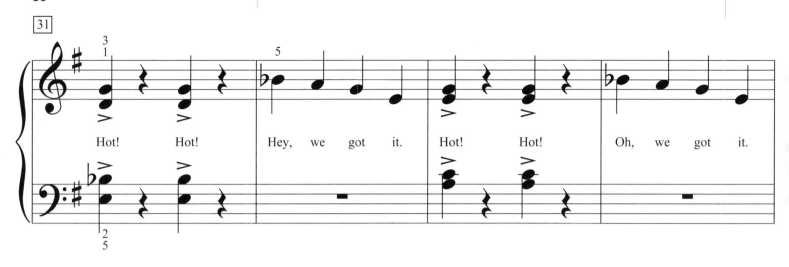

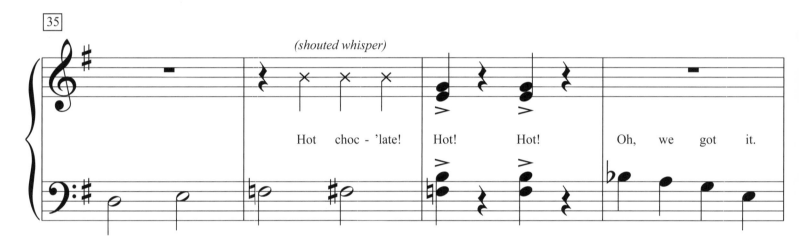

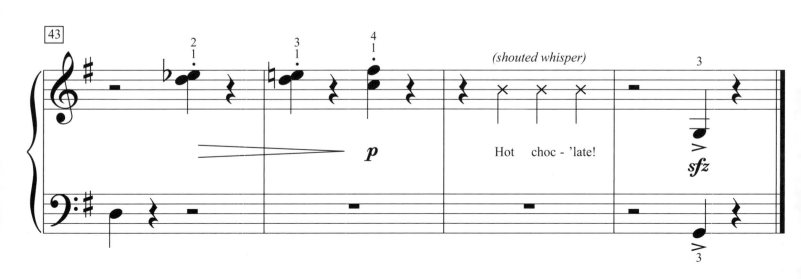

POPULAR SONGS
HAL LEONARD STUDENT PIANO LIBRARY

The **Hal Leonard Student Piano Library** has great songs, and you will find all your favorites here: Disney classics, Broadway and movie favorites, and today's top hits. These graded collections are skillfully and imaginatively arranged for students and pianists at every level, from elementary solos with teacher accompaniments to sophisticated piano solos for the advancing pianist.

Adele
arr. Mona Rejino
00159590 Correlates with HLSPL Level 5..........$12.99

The Beatles
arr. Eugénie Rocherolle
00296649 Correlates with HLSPL Level 5 ....$10.99

Irving Berlin Piano Duos
arr. Don Heitler and Jim Lyke
00296838 Correlates with HLSPL Level 5..........$14.99

Broadway Favorites
arr. Phillip Keveren
00279192 Correlates with HLSPL Level 4..........$12.99

Broadway Hits
arr. Carol Klose
00296650 Correlates with HLSPL Levels 4/5.......$8.99

Chart Hits
arr. Mona Rejino
00296710 Correlates with HLSPL Level 5............$8.99

Christmas Cheer
arr. Phillip Keveren
00296616 Correlates with HLSPL Level 4............$8.99

Classic Christmas Favorites
arr. Jennifer & Mike Watts
00129582 Correlates with HLSPL Level 5............$9.99

Christmas Time Is Here
arr. Eugénie Rocherolle
00296614 Correlates with HLSPL Level 5............$8.99

Classic Joplin Rags
arr. Fred Kern
00296743 Correlates with HLSPL Level 5............$9.99

**Classical Pop –
Lady Gaga Fugue & Other Pop Hits**
arr. Giovanni Dettori
00296921 Correlates with HLSPL Level 5..........$12.99

Contemporary Movie Hits
arr. by Carol Klose, Jennifer Linn and Wendy Stevens
00296780 Correlates with HLSPL Level 5............$8.99

Contemporary Pop Hits
arr. Wendy Stevens
00296836 Correlates with HLSPL Level 3............$8.99

Country Favorites
arr. Mona Rejino
00296861 Correlates with HLSPL Level 5............$9.99

Current Hits
arr. Mona Rejino
00296768 Correlates with HLSPL Level 5............$8.99

Disney Favorites
arr. Phillip Keveren
00296647 Correlates with HLSPL Levels 3/4.......$9.99

Disney Film Favorites
arr. Mona Rejino
00296809 Correlates with HLSPL Level 5..........$10.99

Easy Christmas Duets
arr. Mona Rejino and Phillip Keveren
00237139 Correlates with HLSPL Level 3/4........$9.99

Easy Disney Duets
arr. Jennifer and Mike Watts
00243727 Correlates with HLSPL Level 4..........$12.99

Four Hands on Broadway
arr. Fred Kern
00146177 Correlates with HLSPL Level 5..........$12.99

Jazz Hits for Piano Duet
arr. Jeremy Siskind
00143248 Correlates with HLSPL Level 5 ....$20.99

Elton John
arr. Carol Klose
00296721 Correlates with HLSPL Level 5............$8.99

Joplin Ragtime Duets
arr. Fred Kern
00296771 Correlates with HLSPL Level 5............$8.99

Jerome Kern Classics
arr. Eugénie Rocherolle
00296577 Correlates with HLSPL Level 5..........$12.99

Movie Blockbusters
arr. Mona Rejino
00232850 Correlates with HLSPL Level 5..........$10.99

Pop Hits for Piano Duet
arr. Jeremy Siskind
00224734 Correlates with HLSPL Level 5..........$12.99

Sing to the King
arr. Phillip Keveren
00296808 Correlates with HLSPL Level 5............$8.99

Smash Hits
arr. Mona Rejino
00284841 Correlates with HLSPL Level 5..........$10.99

Spooky Halloween Tunes
arr. Fred Kern
00121550 Correlates with HLSPL Levels 3/4.......$9.99

Today's Hits
arr. Mona Rejino
00296646 Correlates with HLSPL Level 5............$9.99

Top Hits
arr. Jennifer and Mike Watts
00296894 Correlates with HLSPL Level 5..........$10.99

Top Piano Ballads
arr. Jennifer Watts
00197926 Correlates with HLSPL Level 5..........$10.99

You Raise Me Up
arr. Deborah Brady
00296576 Correlates with HLSPL Levels 2/3.......$7.95

HAL•LEONARD®

7777 W. BLUEMOUND RD. P.O. BOX 13819 MILWAUKEE, WI 53213

Visit our website at **www.halleonard.com**

Prices, contents and availability subject to change without notice. Prices may vary outside the U.S.

THE PHILLIP KEVEREN SERIES

PIANO SOLO

ABBA FOR CLASSICAL PIANO
00156644.............................$14.99

ABOVE ALL
00311024.............................$12.99

BACH MEETS JAZZ
00198473.............................$14.99

THE BEATLES
00306412.............................$16.99

THE BEATLES FOR CLASSICAL PIANO
00312189.............................$14.99

THE BEATLES – RECITAL SUITES
00275876.............................$19.99

BEST PIANO SOLOS
00312546.............................$14.99

BLESSINGS
00156601.............................$12.99

BLUES CLASSICS
00198656.............................$12.99

BROADWAY'S BEST
00310669.............................$14.99

A CELTIC CHRISTMAS
00310629.............................$12.99

THE CELTIC COLLECTION
00310549.............................$12.95

CELTIC SONGS WITH A CLASSICAL FLAIR
00280571.............................$12.99

CHRISTMAS MEDLEYS
00311414.............................$12.99

CHRISTMAS AT THE MOVIES
00312190.............................$14.99

CHRISTMAS SONGS FOR CLASSICAL PIANO
00233788.............................$12.99

CINEMA CLASSICS
00310607.............................$14.99

CLASSICAL JAZZ
00311083.............................$12.95

COLDPLAY FOR CLASSICAL PIANO
00137779.............................$15.99

DISNEY RECITAL SUITES
00249097.............................$16.99

DISNEY SONGS FOR CLASSICAL PIANO
00311754.............................$16.99

DISNEY SONGS FOR RAGTIME PIANO
00241379.............................$16.99

THE FILM SCORE COLLECTION
00311811.............................$14.99

FOLKSONGS WITH A CLASSICAL FLAIR
00269408.............................$12.99

GOLDEN SCORES
00233789.............................$14.99

GOSPEL GREATS
00144351.............................$12.99

GREAT STANDARDS
00311157.............................$12.95

THE HYMN COLLECTION
00311071.............................$12.99

HYMN MEDLEYS
00311349.............................$12.99

HYMNS IN A CELTIC STYLE
00280705.............................$12.99

HYMNS WITH A CLASSICAL FLAIR
00269407.............................$12.99

HYMNS WITH A TOUCH OF JAZZ
00311249.............................$12.99

JINGLE JAZZ
00310762.............................$14.99

BILLY JOEL FOR CLASSICAL PIANO
00175310.............................$15.99

ELTON JOHN FOR CLASSICAL PIANO
00126449.............................$15.99

LET FREEDOM RING!
00310839.............................$12.99

ANDREW LLOYD WEBBER
00313227.............................$15.99

MANCINI MAGIC
00313523.............................$14.99

MORE DISNEY SONGS FOR CLASSICAL PIANO
00312113.............................$15.99

MOTOWN HITS
00311295.............................$12.95

PIAZZOLLA TANGOS
00306870.............................$15.99

QUEEN FOR CLASSICAL PIANO
00156645.............................$15.99

RICHARD RODGERS CLASSICS
00310755.............................$15.99

SHOUT TO THE LORD!
00310699.............................$14.99

SONGS FROM CHILDHOOD FOR EASY CLASSICAL PIANO
00233688.............................$12.99

THE SOUND OF MUSIC
00119403.............................$14.99

SYMPHONIC HYMNS FOR PIANO
00224738.............................$14.99

TIN PAN ALLEY
00279673.............................$12.99

TREASURED HYMNS FOR CLASSICAL PIANO
00312112.............................$14.99

THE TWELVE KEYS OF CHRISTMAS
00144926.............................$12.99

YULETIDE JAZZ
00311911.............................$17.99

EASY PIANO

AFRICAN-AMERICAN SPIRITUALS
00310610.............................$10.99

CATCHY SONGS FOR PIANO
00218387.............................$12.99

CELTIC DREAMS
00310973.............................$10.95

CHRISTMAS CAROLS FOR EASY CLASSICAL PIANO
00233686.............................$12.99

CHRISTMAS POPS
00311126.............................$14.99

CLASSIC POP/ROCK HITS
00311548.............................$12.95

A CLASSICAL CHRISTMAS
00310769.............................$10.95

CLASSICAL MOVIE THEMES
00310975.............................$12.99

CONTEMPORARY WORSHIP FAVORITES
00311805.............................$14.99

DISNEY SONGS FOR EASY CLASSICAL PIANO
00144352.............................$12.99

EARLY ROCK 'N' ROLL
00311093.............................$12.99

GEORGE GERSHWIN CLASSICS
00110374.............................$12.99

GOSPEL TREASURES
00310805.............................$12.99

THE VINCE GUARALDI COLLECTION
00306821.............................$16.99

HYMNS FOR EASY CLASSICAL PIANO
00160294.............................$12.99

IMMORTAL HYMNS
00310798.............................$12.99

JAZZ STANDARDS
00311294.............................$12.99

LOVE SONGS
00310744.............................$12.99

THE MOST BEAUTIFUL SONGS FOR EASY CLASSICAL PIANO
00233740.............................$12.99

POP STANDARDS FOR EASY CLASSICAL PIANO
00233739.............................$12.99

RAGTIME CLASSICS
00311293.............................$10.95

SONGS FROM CHILDHOOD FOR EASY CLASSICAL PIANO
00233688.............................$12.99

SONGS OF INSPIRATION
00103258.............................$12.99

TIMELESS PRAISE
00310712.............................$12.95

10,000 REASONS
00126450.............................$14.99

TV THEMES
00311086.............................$12.99

21 GREAT CLASSICS
00310717.............................$12.99

WEEKLY WORSHIP
00145342.............................$16.99

BIG-NOTE PIANO

CHILDREN'S FAVORITE MOVIE SONGS
00310838.............................$12.99

CHRISTMAS MUSIC
00311247.............................$10.95

CLASSICAL FAVORITES
00277368.............................$12.99

CONTEMPORARY HITS
00310907.............................$12.99

DISNEY FAVORITES
00277370.............................$14.99

JOY TO THE WORLD
00310888.............................$10.95

THE NUTCRACKER
00310908.............................$10.99

STAR WARS
00277371.............................$16.99

BEGINNING PIANO SOLOS

AWESOME GOD
00311202.............................$12.99

CHRISTIAN CHILDREN'S FAVORITES
00310837.............................$12.99

CHRISTMAS FAVORITES
00311246.............................$10.95

CHRISTMAS TIME IS HERE
00311334.............................$12.99

CHRISTMAS TRADITIONS
00311117.............................$10.99

EASY HYMNS
00311250.............................$12.99

EVERLASTING GOD
00102710.............................$10.99

JAZZY TUNES
00311403.............................$10.95

PIANO DUET

CLASSICAL THEME DUETS
00311350.............................$10.99

HYMN DUETS
00311544.............................$12.99

PRAISE & WORSHIP DUETS
00311203.............................$12.99

STAR WARS
00119405.............................$14.99

WORSHIP SONGS FOR TWO
00253545.............................$12.99

HAL•LEONARD®

Visit **www.halleonard.com**
for a complete series listing.

Prices, contents, and availability subject to change without notice.